A GIFT FOR

....

FROM

....

This Is No
Fairy Tale

Illustrations by Corbert Gauthier

Dale Tolmasoff

CROSSWAY

A PUBLISHING MINISTRY OF GOOD NEWS PUBLISHERS · WHEATON, ILLINOIS

This Is No Fairy Tale

Text copyright © 2005 by Dale Tolmasoff
Illustrations copyright © by Corbert Gauthier

Published by Crossway Books
A ministry of Good News Publishers
1300 Crescent Street
Wheaton, Illinois 60187

Design: The DesignWorks Group, www.thedesignworksgroup.com
Illustrations by Corbert Gauthier
Cover illustration: Stephen Gardner, Spot art by Corbert Gauthier

First printing, 2005

Printed in Singapore

ISBN 1-58134-644-1

LIBRARY OF CONGRESS CATALOGING-IN-PUBLICATION DATA

Tolmasoff, Dale, 1963-
This is no fairy tale / by Dale Tolmasoff ; illustrations by Corbert Gauthier.
p. cm.
ISBN 1-58134-644-1 (hc : alk. paper)
1. Jesus Christ--Biography--Juvenile literature. I. Gauthier,
Corbert. II. Title.

BT302.T65 2005
232.9'5--dc22

2005002287

To

TOM AND JULIE STELLER
and their children Katie, Nate, and Emma
with my love

FOREWORD

The story you are about to read is unlike any other story in the world. It's a story full of surprises. It's better than any fairy tale you have ever heard. Jesus broke all the rules for fairy-tale kings who try to look real but really aren't. He was poor. He worked with his hands. He played with children. He served the needy. His friends deserted him. And he was killed. But he rose from the dead and is alive today. Nobody ever spoke like Jesus. Nobody ever lived like Jesus. Nobody ever died like Jesus. Not even in fairy tales. And nobody ever rose from the dead like Jesus.

This is a wonderful story. But what makes this story so important is that it is true. It is not a fairy tale. It really happened. You can believe it and build your whole life on it. Come, let's read it together.

JOHN PIPER

We all love to hear fairy tales, don't we?
They are always filled with exciting adventures. But we know
that they are just pretend. This story is very different.
It really happened. The Bible says that a long time ago,
God, the one who created all things, decided to become a real human
person, just like us. His name was Jesus.
He came to live with people because he loved us so much
and wanted to show us what God was really like.
Doesn't that sound wonderful? But some people think it sounds *too*
wonderful. They think it must be just another fairy tale.
How can we be sure it really happened?

If this were a fairy tale, Jesus would have been born in a big castle in a great kingdom. His parents would have been the king and queen, and all the people in the kingdom would have celebrated the birth of the new prince.

The truth is, Jesus was born to a poor family in a small country. In fact, he wasn't even born in a house, but in a stable where animals are kept. And no one even knew about it except a few shepherds who came to see him.

If this were a fairy tale,

the young prince Jesus would have been taught to rule
over people so that when he grew up,
he would become their king.

The truth is,

Jesus learned to work hard with his hands.
His father taught him how to make things for
people out of wood.

If this were a fairy tale,

King Jesus would be too important to talk with little children.
The only chance they would have to see him would be
when he rode by in his horse-drawn carriage.

The truth is,

Jesus loved to spend time with children.
He was very kind and taught them
many things.

If this were a fairy tale,
Jesus would have many servants in the castle
to take care of him and do whatever he wanted.

The truth is, Jesus served other people.
Many times he did wonderful miracles to heal sick people.
He made blind people see again. He made lame people walk again.
He even brought dead people back to life.
There is nothing that Jesus couldn't do for those he loved.

If this were a fairy tale, King Jesus would be very, very rich. He would own beautiful houses and land and horses and clothes. Inside his castle he would have a big room filled with so much gold and treasure that he could buy everything he ever wanted.

The truth is, Jesus was a poor man. He loved doing the work of God so much that he didn't think much about money and the things he could buy. He didn't have fancy clothes to wear or even a house to sleep in. He didn't have a horse to ride. Instead, he had to borrow a donkey from someone else to ride into the city.

If this were a fairy tale,
Jesus' people would always be loyal to him.
If an enemy ever tried to hurt him,
they would fight to protect their king.

The truth is,
one of Jesus' friends told his enemies where they
could catch him. When soldiers came to arrest Jesus,
his other friends were afraid and ran away.

If this were a fairy tale,
King Jesus would have lived a long life
and died in his bed surrounded by his family and friends.

The truth is,
when Jesus was still a young man the people killed him.
They treated him like a criminal, even though he was good.
Isn't that terrible?

If this were a fairy tale,
Jesus would be the leader of a large army of soldiers.
He would rule over many lands by conquering them in battle.
He would fight to save his people from their enemies.

The truth is, Jesus came to teach people about the
Kingdom of God. He didn't come to fight wars.
He came to save people from their sins. Jesus was not the kind
of fairy-tale leader they wanted. So they killed him.

If this were a fairy tale,
Jesus' grave would be very large and fancy.
People would come and bring flowers, showing how
much they loved their king.

The truth is, he was buried in a cave. And when
Jesus' friends came there, they saw it was empty! Do you know
what happened? Jesus came back to life again and showed himself
to his friends to prove that everything he said was true.

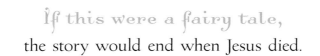

If this were a fairy tale,
the story would end when Jesus died.

The truth is,
this story is still going on.
Jesus is alive right now in heaven with his friends.
And the best part is that you and I can be part of the story.
If we love Jesus and want him to be our king, we can be his friends
too and one day live with him forever. Would you like that?

If you and I trust in Jesus,
this story will turn out much better than a fairy tale for us.
We really will live happily ever after!